Biblical Creation Stories

Biblical Creation Stories

Plural Ways to Nourish Spirituality

MARK G. BOYER

RESOURCE *Publications* · Eugene, Oregon

BIBLICAL CREATION STORIES
Plural Ways to Nourish Spirituality

Copyright © 2025 Mark G. boyer. All rights reserved. Except for brief quotations in critical publications or reviews, no part of this book may be reproduced in any manner without prior written permission from the publisher. Write: Permissions, Wipf and Stock Publishers, 199 W. 8th Ave., Suite 3, Eugene, OR 97401.

Resource Publications
An Imprint of Wipf and Stock Publishers
199 W. 8th Ave., Suite 3
Eugene, OR 97401

www.wipfandstock.com

PAPERBACK ISBN: 979-8-3852-4908-4
HARDCOVER ISBN: 979-8-3852-4909-1
EBOOK ISBN: 979-8-3852-4910-7

VERSION NUMBER 06/24/25

The scripture quotations contained herein are from the *New Revised Standard Version Bible* (NRSV), copyright © 1989 by the Division of Christian Education of the National Council of the Churches of Christ in the U.S.A., and are used by permission. All right reserved.

The scripture quotations contained herein are from the *New Revised Standard Version Updated Edition* (NRSVue), copyright © 2021 National Council of the Churches of Christ in the United States of America. Used by permission. All rights reserved worldwide.

Scripture taken from *The Message: Catholic/Ecumenical Edition* (TM), Copyright © 1993, 1994, 1995, 1996, 2000, 2001, 2002, 2013. Used by permission of NavPress Publishing Group.

The world is charged with the grandeur of God. / It will flame out, like shining from shook foil.

—Gerard Manly Hopkins, *God's Grandeur*

Contents

Abbreviations | ix

    Introduction | xiii
1. In the Beginning | 1
2. Image of God | 13
3. Creator of All | 22
4. Creation Destroyed | 28
5. Something Old, Something New | 33

Recent Books by Mark G. Boyer Published by Wipf & Stock | 41

Abbreviations

Bibles

NRSV = New Revised Standard Version
NRSVue = New Revised Standard Version updated edition
TM = The Message: Catholic/Ecumenical Edition

BCE = Before the Common Era (same as BC = Before Christ)

CB (NT) = Christian Bible (New Testament)

Col = Letter to the Colossians
1 Cor = First Letter of Paul to the Corinthians
Eph = Letter to the Ephesians
Gal = Letter of Paul to the Galatians
Heb = Letter to the Hebrews
John = John's Gospel
Mark = Mark's Gospel
Matt = Matthew's Gospel
2 Pet = Second Letter of Peter
Rev = Revelation
2 Thess = Second Letter to the Thessalonians
1 Tim = First Letter to Timothy

CE = Common Era (same as AD = *Anno Domini*, in the year of the Lord)

HB (OT) = Hebrew Bible (Old Testament)

Amos = Amos
2 Chr = Second Book of Chronicles
Dan = Daniel
Deut = Deuteronomy
Exod = Exodus
Ezek = Ezekiel
Gen = Genesis
Hag = Haggai
Hos = Hosea
Isa = Isaiah
Jer = Jeremiah
Joel = Joel
Judg = Judges
1 Kgs = First Book of Kings
2 Kgs = Second Book of Kings
Mal = Malachi
Mic = Micah
Num = Numbers
Prov = Proverbs
Ps(s) = Psalm(s)
Song = Song of Songs

OT (A) = Old Testament (Apocrypha)

Bel = Bel and the Dragon
1 Esd = First Book of Esdras
2 Esd = Second Book of Esdras
4 Esd = Fourth Book of Esdras
Jdt = Judith
3 Macc = Third Book of Maccabees
Sir = Sirach (Ecclesiasticus)
Wis = Wisdom (of Solomon)

par(s) = paragraph(s)

Punctuation Usage

/ = indicates where one line of poetic text ends and another begins
(biblical notation) = see the specific biblical verse(s) in parentheses for more information
– = range of verses following a colon (8:3–4)
— = range of verses from a verse in one chapter to a verse in another chapter (8:3—9:4)
a, b, c = designates first (a), second (b), third (c), etc. sentence in a verse of Scripture or a line of poetic text

Introduction

TITLE

Biblical Creation Stories

The Bible has multiple creation accounts. Most people know or have heard of the one which took six days, but they are not familiar with the rest. Biblical creation stories are plural because they are hypothetical inventions by various biblical authors. Biblical creation accounts are not science reports based on observable phenomena; they are theories based on varieties of evidence and as interpreted by biblical writers. Even scientific accounts of creation are plural because they are hypotheses based on geologic evidence as interpreted by scientists. The simple fact of the matter is that there was no one present when creation occurred. Thus, with no first-hand experience, various biblical authors—each with his own biases and politics—wrote one. For example, the first two chapters of the HB (OT) book of Genesis features two creation stories back-to-back. The first one is focused on the seventh day being a day of rest from work founded on the seven days in a week mythology; the second one is focused on the creation of people.

Biblical creation stories are about the act of God creating and the product of that creation. To use another word, all biblical creation stories are myths; they attempt to explain why things are the way they are. Thus, for example, why is there a large sun and a small moon that cross under the dome of the sky every day? The creation mythology states that God created the sun to produce light during the day, and he created the moon to produce light during the night. Likewise, there is the myth that there are seven days in a week because God created for six days and rested on the seventh day. Neither of those answers are scientific; both are based on human experience in order to answer the question about why the sun shines during the day and the moon during the night and why there are seven days in a week.

SUBTITLE

Plural Ways to Nourish Spirituality

While it is not exhaustive, this book explores the many biblical creation stories and invites readers to use them to nourish their spirituality. Spirituality is the experience of the human spirit connecting to the divine Spirit, or vice-versa. Through reading the plurality of biblical texts about creation, through reflections on creation accounts, through praying a part of a Psalm, through meditating on a question designed to lead the reader into deeper reflection based on his or her personal life, and through journaling to record insights, a reader can nourish his or her spirituality. Insights can be gained that strengthen the Spirit-spirit connection.

USING THIS BOOK

Biblical Creation Stories consists of twenty-five exercises gathered into five chapters. Each exercise begins with a passage of Scripture about creation. A Reflection follows, explaining the biblical passage and noting other similar biblical passages and their meanings. The Reflection is followed by a Psalm Response, a few verses from a HB (OT) Psalm that illustrates both the Scripture that began the exercise and the reflection. The exercise concludes with a Meditation/Journal question, whose goal is to prompt the reader to apply the Scripture, Reflection, and Psalm Response to his or her life. The application process is where the Spirit-spirit connection occurs, and it is where a person's spirituality is nourished. Also, at the end of each chapter is a Summary of what was explored about creation in the chapter.

NOTES ON THE BIBLE

Three Parts

The Bible is divided into two parts: The Hebrew Bible (Old Testament) and the Christian Bible (New Testament). The Hebrew Bible consists of thirty-nine named books accepted by Jews and Protestants as Holy Scripture. The Old Testament also contains those thirty-nine books plus seven to eighteen more named books or parts of books called the Apocrypha or the Deuterocanonical Books; the Old Testament is accepted by Catholics and several other Christian denominations as Holy Scripture. The Christian Bible, consisting of twenty-seven named books, is also called the New Testament; it is accepted by Christians as Holy Scripture. Thus, in this work:

—**Hebrew Bible (Old Testament)**, abbreviated **HB (OT)**, indicates that a book is found both in the Hebrew Bible and the Old Testament;

—**Old Testament (Apocrypha)**, abbreviated **OT (A)**, indicates that a book is found only in the Old Testament Apocrypha and not in the Hebrew Bible;

—and **Christian Bible (New Testament)**, abbreviated **CB (NT)**, indicates that a book is found only in the Christian Bible or New Testament.

In notating biblical texts, the first number refers to the chapter in the book, and the second number (following the colon) refers to the verse within the chapter. Thus, HB (OT) Isa 7:11 means that the quotation comes from Isaiah, chapter 7, verse 11. OT (A) Sir 39:30 means that the quotation comes from Sirach, chapter 39, verse 30. CB (NT) Mark 6:2 means that the quotation comes from Mark's Gospel, chapter 6, verse 2. When more than one sentence appears in a verse, the letters a, b, c, etc. indicate the sentence being referenced in the verse. Thus, HB (OT) 2 Kgs 1:6a means that the quotation comes from the Second Book of Kings, chapter 1, verse 6, sentence 1. Also, poetry, such as the Psalms and sections of Judith, Proverbs, Isaiah, and others may be noted using the letters a, b, c, etc. to indicate the lines being used. Thus, Ps 16:4a refers to the first line of verse 4 of Psalm 16; there are two more lines of verse 4: b and c.

In the HB (OT) and the OT (A), the reader often sees LORD (note all capital letters). Because God's name (Yahweh or YHWH, referred to as the Tetragrammaton) is not to be pronounced, the name Adonai (meaning *Lord*) is substituted for Yahweh when a biblical text is read. When a biblical text is translated and printed, LORD (Gen 2:4) is used to alert the reader to what the text actually states: Yahweh. Furthermore, when the biblical author writes Lord Yahweh, printers present Lord GOD (note all capital letters for GOD; Gen 15:2) to avoid the printed ambiguity of LORD LORD. In the Psalms in *The Message*, GOD (note all capital letters) is substituted for Yahweh. When the reference is to Jesus, the word printed is Lord (note capital L and lower-case letters; Luke 11:1). When writing about a lord (note all lower-case letters; Matt 18:25) with servants, no capital L is used.

In this book, *cf.* (meaning *confer*) has not been used. Biblical notations placed in parentheses indicate where the reference can be found in the Bible. For example, the Second Book of Samuel records King David writing a song (2 Sam 22:1–51). The notation in parentheses is given to the reader, who may wish to check the full reference in his or her Bible. In some instances, a few notations appear in parentheses; again, the reader may wish to see the references in their contexts.

Bibles

Most Bible readers are not aware that there is no such thing as the original Bible! The fact is: There are Bibles. First, there is the Jewish Bible, often called the Hebrew Bible; its books were collected and completed between 70 and 90 CE based on the Jerusalem canon (collection) in this order: Torah (Genesis, Exodus, Leviticus, Numbers, Deuteronomy), Prophets (Isaiah, Jeremiah, Ezekiel, etc.), and Writings (Job, Psalms, Proverbs, etc). It is important to note the arrangement of the collected books. Second, there is—for want of a better name—the Christian Hebrew Bible, completed in the fourth century CE, but not defined until after the Reformation. It consists of Torah, Writings, and Prophets. It is important to note the (re)ordering of the collected books. Christianity took the Jewish (Hebrew) Bible and rearranged the order of its books! Then, Christianity named it the Old Testament.

The Jerusalem canon, obviously, is the collection of biblical books used in Jerusalem and its environs. A large community of Jews, however, lived in Alexandria, Egypt. To the Jerusalem canon (books in Hebrew and Aramaic) they added books in Greek, the language they spoke; this collection is the Alexandrine canon. They also translated the Jerusalem canon's books from Hebrew and Aramaic into Greek. That translation, containing books and parts of books not in the Jerusalem canon, is called the Septuagint (abbreviated LXX). Later, the Septuagint was translated into Latin; it is known as the Vulgate. Every time a book of the Bible is translated, it picks up something and it loses something; that is because there is no such thing as literary equivalence. For example, in Greek there are four words for love, but English only has one word for love. Thus, no matter what the Greek word is, it is always translated into English as love.

Thus, we have (1) the Hebrew Bible—the Jewish Bible, (2) the Hebrew Bible (Old Testament)—the rearranged books of the Hebrew Bible, and (3) the Christian Bible—twenty-seven books originally written in Greek. The Protestant Bible contains only the books in the Jerusalem canon, but rearranged into the Old Testament, plus the Christian Bible books; the Catholic Bible contains the books in the Alexandrine collection plus the Christian Bible books.

The extra books or parts of books found in the Catholic Bible (and coming from the Alexandrine collection of the Jewish Bible), but not found in a Protestant Bible, are collectively referred to as the Apocrypha or Deuterocanonical Books. They include Tobit, Judith, additions to Esther, Wisdom of Solomon, Sirach (Ecclesiasticus), Baruch, Letter of Jeremiah, Prayer of Azariah (addition to Daniel), Susanna (addition to Daniel), Bel and the Dragon (addition to Daniel), 1 Maccabees, 2 Maccabees, 1 Esdras, Prayer of Manasseh, Psalm 151, 3 Maccabees, 2 Esdras, and 4 Maccabees. Not every Christian group, such as Catholics, accepts all the books in the Apocrypha as Scripture; for example, out of the four books of Maccabees, Catholics accept only 1 and 2 Maccabees. In Catholic Bibles, the additional books are placed with similar books. Thus, First and Second Maccabees are inserted with the historical books; the books of Wisdom and Sirach are found in the wisdom literature section.

Thus, there is no single or original Bible; there are many Bibles; it depends on what books a specific denomination or group (Jews, Christians) accepts as Scripture. The Bible that contains any book that any group accepts as Scripture is *The Access Bible* (updated edition): *New Revised Standard Version with the Apocrypha*, general editors Gail R. O'Day and David Petersen, published in New York by Oxford University Press in 1999 and updated in 2011. There is also the *New Revised Standard Version updated edition*, published by Zondervan in 2022; however, the latter does not contain the information sidebars found in the former book.

Thus, a Bible reader should keep in mind the following: In a Christian Bible, The Old Testament consists of the rearranged books found in the Hebrew (Jewish) Bible. Roman Catholics and some others add some books and parts of books to that Old Testament because they were found in the Alexandrine collection. In general, Protestants do not add books to the Old Testament; they follow the Jerusalem collection of books, but rearrange them as noted above. Almost all Christians accept the twenty-seven books of the New Testament; there are a few groups that reject one or another of the books in the collection.

Thus, as you can see, this can become difficult to navigate, especially when someone says, "The Bible says . . . ." The astute Bible reader needs to ask, "Which book in which Bible says that?" There is no such thing as the original Bible. There are Bibles, various libraries of books collected over three thousand years by individuals and groups who declared their collection (canon) to be Scripture. When engaged in Bible study, it is also important to note that the Bible is a library of books written by different authors at different times in history; it is not a single book.

Presuppositions

The HB (OT) begins as stories passed on by word of mouth from one person to another. Sometime during the oral transmission stage, authors decided to collect the oral stories and write them. A change occurs immediately. One does not tell a story the same way one writes a story. Repetition and correction occur in oral story-telling. Except for future emendations by copyists, single statements by characters and plot structure dominate written stories. Furthermore, in both oral and written story-telling, types or models are employed. In the HB (OT), for example, Joshua and Elijah are types of Moses. In the CB (NT) Elizabeth becomes a type of Hannah, who is herself a type of Sarah. When orally narrating or writing a story, the teller or author consciously creates one character as a type of another in order to make the character and his or her words and actions intelligible to the hearer or reader.

In the CB (NT) the oldest gospel is Mark's account of Jesus' victory. The author of Matthew's Gospel copied and shortened about eighty percent of Mark's material into his book and then added other stories to make the work longer. The author of Luke's Gospel copied and shortened about fifty percent of Mark's material into his orderly account and then added other stories to make the work much longer. The material shared by Matthew and Luke is called Q—from the German word *Quelle*, meaning *Source*—by biblical scholars. Mark's Gospel begins as oral story-telling, lasting for about forty years in that form. An unidentified author, called Mark for the sake of convenience, collects the oral stories, sets a plot, and writes the first gospel around 70 CE. Because Jesus was expected to return soon, no one had thought about recording what he had said and done until Mark came along and realized that he was not returning as quickly as had been thought. About ten years after Mark finished his gospel, Matthew needed to adopt Mark's narrative—originally intended for a peasant Gentile readership—to a Jewish audience. And about twenty years after Mark finished his gospel, Luke needed to adapt Mark's poor Gentile-intended work for a rich, upper class, urban, Gentile readership. The author of John's Gospel did not know the existence of the other three works collectively named synoptic gospels. A point often overlooked by modern readers is the fact that they are not the intended readers of biblical texts. Every biblical book was written to a specific group of people at a specific time in history. Thus, Paul did not write to people living in the United States; he wrote in Greek to people living in Rome, Corinth, and Thessalonica. Modern readers are reading an English translation (and interpretation) with Roman-Greco cultural presuppositions underlying the text.

Furthermore, letters and gospels were not first intended to be read privately as is done today. They were meant to be heard in a group. The very low rate of literacy in the first century would have never dictated many copies of texts since most people could not read, and their standard practice was to listen to another read the letters and stories to them. Thus, what began as oral story-telling passed on by word of mouth became written story-telling preserved in gospels and letters. A careful reading of Mark's Gospel will reveal the orality still embedded in the text, especially evident in the repetition of words and the organization of stories in three parts. In rewriting Mark, Matthew and Luke remove the last traces of oral story-telling. Paul intended his letters to be read when the community to whom they were addressed gathered.

The letters of Paul are older than the gospels. Biblical scholars divide the letters of Paul into the authentic letters—those written by Paul (Romans, Galatians, Philippians, etc.)—and those written by someone else in Paul's name—second generation Pauline letters (Ephesians, Colossians, Titus, etc.). The latter group of letters usually develop Pauline thought for a new generation of Christians. The reader of letters needs to keep in mind that the letter was not addressed to him or her; it was addressed to a specific group of believers in the mid- to late-first century CE. In addition to the Pauline body of letters, there are other letters that were gathered and placed in the CB (NT) canon (collection), such as James, 1 and 2 Peter, Jude, etc. These anonymous letters were written in the name of an apostle to give them authority in the Christian communities to which they were addressed.

Biblical *C*reation Stories

1

In the Beginning

WHEN?

Scripture: "When God began to create the heavens and the earth, the earth was complete chaos and darkness covered the face of the deep, while a wind from God swept over the face of the waters." (Gen 1:1–2, NRSVue)

Reflection: Many translations of the first verse of the HB (OT) book of Genesis start with "In the beginning" (NRSV). That phrase indicates primordial biblical time; in other words, that phrase points to the time before time began! In a footnote, the NRSV indicates that the Hebrew words could also be translated as "When God began to create," as the NRSVue editors chose after the review of the NRSV from 2017 to 2021. The verses above come from what biblical scholars refer to as the Priestly version of creation, which was written during the captivity of the Jews in Babylon (587–38 BCE) and in dialogue with the National Babylonian creation account, known as Enuma Elish. The Babylonian story presents a battle among the gods with the world being the product of combat and copulation. Marduk agrees to combat Tiamat if all the other gods agree to make him their chief. After beating the goddess, he divides her corpse into the heavens and the earth and establishes times and seasons. After defeating Tiamat's husband, Marduk creates humans from his blood. The authors of Genesis 1 present a counter version of creation in which there is no combat; God, referred to Elohim, crafts a chaotic cosmos into order using only words. The chaos of the deep waters is brought to order by the wind from God; the Hebrew word for wind—*ruah*—can also be translated as *breath* or *spirit*. Like a dove hovering over its nest, God hovers over the chaos and, with his wind, breath, or spirit, creates order. The wind, breath, or spirit of God is fecundity in action. In short order, the chaotic darkness will be turned into light (Gen 1:3); a dome will separate the waters (Gen 1:7), seas and dry land will appear (Gen 1:9), vegetation appears (Gen 1:11), and the sun, moon, and stars are created (Gen 1:16). Then, life begins with sea creatures (Gen 1:21), earth creatures (Gen 1:25), and human creatures (Gen 1:27).

Because humans experience a beginning and an end to all things including themselves, they project that there must be a beginning (and an end) to the world, and such is the Priestly creation account. The Priestly account of creation is the youngest of the two accounts (Gen 1:1—2:3; 2:4–25), and it was appended to the beginning of the HB (OT) book of Genesis during the Babylonian Captivity of the Jews to demonstrate the superiority of their God, who creates with words, to Marduk, who creates with a corpse and blood. It also focuses on the last day of the Babylonian week, called the Sabbath by the Jews and called Saturday by other peoples. The last day of the week is a day of rest in imitation of God, who rested (Gen 2:3). In the words of the OT (A) book of Wisdom, God "created all things so that they might exist; / the generative forces of the world are wholesome" (Wis 1:14ab, NRSVue).

Psalm Response: "God's glory is on tour in the skies, / God-craft on exhibit across the horizon. / Madame Day holds classes every morning, / Professor Night lectures each evening. / Their words aren't heard, / their voices aren't recorded, / But their silence fills the earth; / unspoken truth is spoken everywhere." (Ps 19:1–4, TM)

Meditation/Journal: What unspoken truth have you discovered in the Scripture passage or Reflection above?

IN THE DAY

Scripture: "In the day that the LORD God made the earth and the heavens, when no plant of the field was yet in the earth and no vegetation of the field had yet sprung up—for the LORD God had not caused it to rain upon the earth, and there was no one to till the ground, but a stream would rise from the earth and water the whole face of the ground." (Gen 2:4b–6, NRSVue)

Reflection: The second account of creation found in the Bible (Gen 2:4—25) begins with a barren earth. Nothing was growing, because Yahweh (LORD) had not sent rain, and, even if he had, there was no human on the earth to prepare it for growth. Thus, according to the older account of creation, the LORD God, like a potter at a wheel, creates a person from the soil and breathes into (inspirits) him (with) life. Then, God plants a garden, Eden, and fills it with tree-bearing fruit. Then, Yahweh creates animals, and, after he puts the man into a deep sleep, takes one of the man's ribs and fashions a woman from it (Gen 2:21). She is, literally, bone of his bones and flesh of his flesh. The author of the OT (A) book of Wisdom disagrees with the oldest story of creation. He writes that the Lord's "all-powerful hand / . . . created the world out of formless matter" (Wis 11:17ab, NRSVue).

The first story of creation referred to the deity as God; the second story refers to the deity as LORD God, indicating a different author than the first account. LORD is what Bible translators use to indicate that the text states *Yahweh* or *Yhwh*, the name that is not pronounced. The author of the first account of creation envisions God being a member of the assembly of divine beings, whereas the older account (labeled the J tradition by scholars), written before the 587 BCE Babylonian exile, presumes that he alone rules the world. The dry desert of this account, a sign of chaos, is not the watery chaos of the first account. The LORD God spins his potter's wheel, and from the mud (*adamah*) he shapes the man (*adam*), giving him life by breathing into (inspiriting) him. Then, the LORD God plants a garden, named Eden (delight), and gives it to the man to till and keep. Noticing that the man (*ish*) needs help, the LORD God creates woman (*ishshah*). The experience of the biblical writer dictated that a woman was needed for the man to reproduce; thus, in biblical culture the man, who carries the seed of new life, needs an incubator in which to plant the seed until it grows into a new person. The fact that the agricultural imagery suggests that this earlier account came from a farming community should not be overlooked.

Psalm Response: "GOD, brilliant Lord, / yours is a household name. / I look up at your macro-skies, dark and enormous, / your handmade sky-jewelry, / Moon and stars mounted in their settings. / Then I look at my micro-self and wonder, / Why do you bother with us? Why take a second look our way? / You put us in charge of your handcrafted world, / repeated to us your Genesis-charge, / Made us lords of sheep and cattle, / even animals out in the wild, / Birds flying and fish swimming, / whales singing in the ocean deeps." (Ps 8:1, 3–4, 6–8, TM)

Journal/Meditation: What new truth about creation have you discovered in the Scripture passage or Reflection above?

BEFORE THE BEGINNING

Scripture: "The LORD created me at the beginning of his work, / the first of his acts of long ago. / Ages ago I was set up, / at the first, before the beginning of the earth. / . . . [W]hen he marked out the foundations of the earth, / then I was beside him, like a master worker, / and I was daily his delight, / playing before him always . . . ." (Prov 8:22–23, 29b–30, NRSVue)

Reflection: In biblical wisdom literature, wisdom is personified as a woman, who was created by the LORD before he began to create, as the author of the HB (OT) book of Proverbs states, "before the beginning of the earth." The author of the book dialogues with the Genesis creation stories, presupposing that there was a time when wisdom was created and functioned like a primordial architect. Thus, before there were depths or springs (Prov 8:24), before there were mountains or hills (Prov 8:25), before there were earth, fields, or soil (Prov 8:26), before there were heavens, seas, or skies (Prov 8:27–28), before the earth's foundations were prepared (Prov 8:29), wisdom stood beside the LORD, holding the architectural plans in her hands.

Personified Lady Wisdom speaks; she tells the tale of her origin, sovereignly made before God did anything else. She raises the reader's awareness as to the importance of wisdom, which is understood to be good sense, the knowledge and experience needed to make sensible decisions and judgments. If God used wisdom to create, then those who follow the LORD should seek her throughout their lives. "Lay aside immaturity and live," she states, "and walk in the way of insight" (Prov 9:6, NRSVue).

Psalm Response: "What a wildly wonderful world, GOD! / You made it all, with Wisdom at your side, / made earth overflow with your wonderful creations. / The glory of GOD—let it last forever! / Let GOD enjoy his creation! / Oh, let me sing to GOD all my life long, / sing hymns to my God as long as I live! / Oh, let my song please him; / I'm so pleased to be singing to GOD." (Ps 104:24, 31, 33–34, TM)

Journal/Meditation: On a scale of one to five, where do you place your wisdom? What examples can you give to support your answer?

CREATOR LORD (YAHWEH)

Scripture: "Thus says God, the LORD, / who created the heavens and stretched them out, / who spread out the earth and what comes from it, / who gives breath to the people upon it / and spirit to those who walk in it: / I am the LORD; I have called you in righteousness; / I have taken you by the hand and kept you; / I have given you as a covenant to the people, a light to the nations . . . ." (Isa 42:5–6, NRSVue)

Reflection: Chapters forty through fifty-five of the HB (OT) book of the prophet Isaiah are called Second Isaiah by biblical scholars. Those chapters were written after 538 BCE, after the Mede and Persian forces had defeated Babylon; they were prepared by a prophet, who gives the hope of returning to Jerusalem to the Jews. The prophet declares, ". . . [T]he Lord GOD comes with might" (Isa 40:10a, NRSVue). The prophet asks his readers: "Who has measured the waters of the sea in the hollow of his hand / and marked off the heavens with a span, / enclosed the dust of the earth in a measure / and weighed the mountains in scales / and the hills in a balance?" (Isa 40:12, NRSVue). The reader must answer: "The LORD God." Even though the author of the HB (OT) book of Proverbs presents Wisdom as God's master worker, Isaiah asks, "Who has directed the spirit of the LORD / or as his counselor has instructed him? / Whom did he consult for his enlightenment . . . ?" (Isa 40:13–14a, NRSVue) The reader is supposed to answer, "No one." Then, Second Isaiah states his presumption that the world was created like a three-storied building. From the perspective of God, "who sits above the circle of the earth," "who stretches out the heavens like a curtain / and spreads them like a tent to live in" / the earth's "inhabitants [look] like grasshoppers" on the earth's second level (Isa 40:22, NRSVue). Not mentioned by Second Isaiah here is Sheol, the third level of the universe.

"Who created these?" asks Second Isaiah (40:26b, NRSVue). Then he answers, "The LORD is the everlasting God, / the Creator of the ends of the earth." (Isa 40:28b, NRSVue). In other words, ". . . [T]he hand of the LORD has done this, / the Holy One of Israel has created it" (Isa 41:20cd, NRSVue). Later, Second Isaiah portrays God stating, "I form light and create darkness, / I make weal and create woe; / I the LORD do all these things. / I made the earth / and created humankind upon it; / it was my hands that stretched out the heavens . . . . / For thus says the LORD, / who created the heavens (he is God!), / who formed the earth and made it (he established it; / he did not create it a chaos; / he formed it to be inhabited): I am the LORD, and there is no other" (Isa 45:7, 12, 18, NRSVue). Thus, according to Second Isaiah, the

LORD (Yahweh) God created the heavens and the earth, and he intended that they be inhabited.

Psalm Response: "Good people, cheer GOD! / Invent your own new song to him; / give him a trumpet fanfare. / For GOD's Word is solid to the core; / everything he makes is sound inside and out. / He loves it when everything fits, / when his world is in plumb-line true. / Earth is drenched / in GOD's affectionate satisfaction. / The skies were made by GOD's command; / he breathed the word and the stars popped out. / He scooped Sea into his jug, / put Ocean in his keg." (Ps 33:1, 3–7, TM)

Journal/Meditation: What psalm (song) might you write praising the LORD God as creator?

THE LORD CREATED WISDOM

Scripture: "It is [the Lord] who created [wisdom]; / he saw her and took her measure; / he poured her out upon all his works." (Sir 1:9, NRSVue)

Reflection: The biblical author of the OT (A) book of Sirach agrees with the biblical author of the OT (HB) book of Proverbs. "Wisdom was created before all things," writes the author of Sirach, "and prudent understanding from eternity" (Sir 1:4, NRSVue). In a section of his book where "wisdom praises herself" (Sir 24:1a, NRSVue), personified Wisdom declares: "I came forth from the mouth of the Most High / and covered the earth like a mist. I encamped in the heights, / and my throne was in a pillar of cloud." (Sir 24:3–4, NRSVue). Emphasizing that she was created before anything else, Lady Wisdom declares, "Before the ages, in the beginning, he created me, / and for all the ages I shall not cease to be" (Sir 24:9, NRSVue). Since Wisdom has existed before there was time, the author of the book of Sirach can declare, "The Lord apportioned to [our ancestors in their generations] great glory, his majesty from the beginning" (Sir 44:2, NRSVue).

Echoing the above Scripture passage and echoing God's ordering of chaos in the HB (OT) book of Genesis, Sirach states, "When the Lord created his works from the beginning / and, in making them, determined their boundaries, / he arranged their works in an eternal order / and their dominion for all generations" (Sir 16:26–27ab, NRSVue). This leads the author to conclude, "No one can say, 'What is this?' or 'Why is that?'—/ for everything has been created for its own purpose" (Sir 39:21, NRSVue). God poured wisdom into everything he made.

Prayer Response: "There's no God but you, Lord. Create new signage; do new wonders. . . . [Y]our storied wonders need to be made known.

Reintroduce the prophets, who were your creations; breathe new life into the prophecies they spoke in your name. Reward those who've kept their faith intact; may they find your word still relevant. Hear the prayers of your servants; be gracious to us as you promised . . . ." (Sir 36:5b–6, 10b, 20–21, NRSVue)

Journal/Meditation: Make a list of things that you consider to be created for their own purpose. Where do you see wisdom inherent in each item?

ESDRAS ON CREATION

Scripture: "[The angel Uriel] said to me [, Ezra], 'At the beginning of the circle of the earth, before the portals of the world were in place, and before the assembled winds blew, and before the rumblings of thunder sounded, and before the flashes of lightning shone, and before the foundations of paradise were laid, and before the beautiful flowers were seen, and before the powers of movements were established, and before the innumerable hosts of angels were gathered together, and before the heights of the air were lifted up, and before the measures of the firmaments were named . . . , and before the present years were reckoned . . . —then I planned these things, and they were made through me alone and not through another . . . ." (2 Esd 6:1—6, NRSVue)

Reflection: In the OT (A) book of Second Esdras, there appears the above account of creation. The angel (a biblical way for God to speak) Uriel (whose name means *light of God* or *fire of God*) tells Ezra about the beginning of creation, referred to as the circle of the earth, because that is how it was imagined. The portals are the floodgates located in the dome over the earth. The winds, thunder, and lightning were, imaginatively, kept in storehouses located above the dome. Paradisial flat-plate-like earth rested on seven foundation pillars. God planned and made all of creation—height and depth—before flowers, roads, and angels existed and before the counting of years began.

Before this, Ezra wanted to know why God did not create at one time those who have been and those who are and those who will be (2 Esd 5:43). He received the reply that creation cannot move faster than the Creator, nor could the world hold at one time all those created in it (2 Esd 5:44). Ezra hypothesizes that because God gives life to all at one time, creation might be able to support all life that was, is, and will be (2 Esd 5:45–46). As far as the Creator is concerned, creation is an ongoing process (2 Esd 5:49). Later in the book, Ezra rehearses the six days of creation as it is found at the beginning of the HB (OT) book of Genesis. Heaven and earth are made on the first day (2 Esd 6:38–40); the firmament that separates the waters below from those above on the second day (2 Esd 6:41); dry land on the third day (2 Esd 6:42–44); the sun, moon, and stars on the fourth day (2 Esd 6:45–46); living creatures on the fifth day (2 Esd 6:47–52); and animals and Adam on the sixth day (2 Esd 6:53–54). The author states "that it was for [the Jews] that [the Lord] created this world" (2 Esd 6:55, NRSVue).

Prayer Response: "All this I [, Ezra,] have spoken before you, O Lord, because you have said that it was for us that you created this world. As for the other nations that have descended from Adam, you have said that they are nothing and that they are like spittle, and you have compared their abundance to a drop from a bucket. And now, O Lord, these nations, which are reputed to be as nothing, domineer over us and devour us. But we your people, whom you have called your firstborn, only begotten, zealous for you, and most dear, have been given into their hands. If the world has indeed been created for us, why do we not possess our world as an inheritance? How long will this be so?" (2 Esd 6:55–59, NRSVue)

Meditation/Journal: According to the Second Book of Esdras, what was the purpose of creation? According to Ezra's prayer (Prayer Response) what was the purpose of creation? What do you think was the purpose of creation?

FROM THE BEGINNING

Scripture: While sitting on the Mount of Olives opposite the temple, Jesus said to Peter, James, John, and Andrew: ". . . [W]hen you see the desolating sacrilege set up where it ought not to be (let the reader understand), then those in Judea must flee to the mountains; the one on the housetop must not go down or enter to take anything from the house; the one in the field must not turn back to get a coat. Woe to those who are pregnant and to those who are nursing infants in those days! Pray that it may not be in winter. For in those days there will be suffering, such as has not been from the beginning of the creation that God created until now and never will be." (Mark 13:14–19, NRSVue)

Reflection: While one would not expect to find a reference to creation in the CB (NT), the author of Mark's Gospel presents Jesus referring to it. The Markan Jesus' words are located in what biblical scholars refer to as the Little Apocalypse, chapter 13 of Mark's Gospel. Apocalyptic is a type of literature with a pessimistic view of the world, that contains a dualistic outlook separating people into the saved and the damned, and descriptions of future events to be endured. In chapter 13 of Mark's Gospel, Jesus reflects on the destruction of the temple with some of his apostles. Historically, the Romans destroyed the second temple in 70 CE; by portraying his Jesus character predicting the destruction of it, the author of Mark's Gospel gives Jesus the authority to know the future (no writer would ever present a character predicting the future if the event had not already happened!). The "desolating sacrilege" refers to an event found in the HB (OT) book of Daniel with more information from the OT (A) First Book of Maccabees (1:54): King Antiochus Epiphanes, a Greek ruler after the death of Alexander the Great, attempted to Hellenize the Jews by building a pagan altar on the one in the temple and slaughtering swine on it. His action led to a Jewish revolt with a war that, for a time, drove the Greek overlords out of Jerusalem and Judea. The author of Mark's Gospel expected the Romans to imitate the Greeks by establishing a statue in the temple after 70 CE. The phrase "(let the reader understand)" is a message to the person reading aloud this part of Mark's Gospel after 70 CE. When the Romans attacked Jerusalem in 70 CE, many of the city's inhabitants fled to the mountains to escape the slaughter; they were urged to move quickly and not be concerned grabbing anything from their homes. Pregnant women and those with nursing infants found flight from Jerusalem to be hard during the winter of 67–68 CE. The suffering the Romans inflicted on the inhabitants of Jerusalem was fresh in the experience of the readers of Mark's Gospel; they described it as such intense suffering that had not ever been experienced from the beginning of creation when God created. After besieging Jerusalem for a long time, the city fell, and the Romans destroyed its walls and its temple and scattered its population or caused its population to flee the destruction.

The author of Matthew's Gospel, writing (80 CE) about ten years after Mark's Gospel was written (70 CE), transforms Mark's Little Apocalypse into signs that followers of Jesus of Nazareth are living according to Jesus' teaching. The author of Matthew's Gospel interprets his Markan material about the desolating sacrilege as a reference to the prophet Daniel (Matt 24:15). The author of Matthew's Gospel understands that persecution awaits Jesus' followers. ". . . [T]here will be great suffering, such as has not been from the beginning of the world until now, no, and never will be" (Matt 24:21, NRSVue). However, Matthew's readers have a mission to proclaim the kingdom of God throughout the world (Matt 24:14). The author of this gospel speaks of the recent past (as he found it recorded in Mark's Gospel) and applies it to his own present experiences, which, indeed, are dark and imagined to be so great as to challenge any suffering that has occurred to people since the beginning of the world. (Let the reader understand that the author of Luke's Gospel does not record the material about suffering he found in Mark's Gospel.)

Canticle Response: "Heavens, raise the roof! Earth, wake the dead! / Mountains, send up cheers! / GOD has comforted his people. / He has tenderly nursed his beaten-up, beaten down people. / 'Can a mother forget the infant at her beast, / walk away from the baby she bore? / But even if mothers forget, / I'd never forget you—never. / Look, I've written your names on the backs of my hands.'" (Isa 49:13, 15–16a TM)

Journal/Meditation: What intense or extreme suffering have you endured? In what specific way(s) do you interpret it (apply meaning to it) for your life?

REMOVAL OF CREATED THINGS

Scripture: "See that you do not refuse the one who is speaking, for if they did not escape when they refused the one who warned them on earth, how much less will we escape if we reject the one who warns from heaven! At that time his voice shook the earth, but now he has promised, 'Yet once more I will shake not only the earth but also the heaven.' This phrase, 'Yet once more,' indicates the removal of what is shaken—that is, created things—so that what cannot be shaken may remain. Therefore, since we are receiving a kingdom that cannot be shaken, let us show gratitude, by which we may offer to God an acceptable worship with reverence and awe, for indeed our God is a consuming fire." (Heb 12:25–29, NRSVue)

Reflection: The last five verses of chapter 12 of the CB (NT) Letter to the Hebrews presents a warning to the readers that is based on a quotation from the HB (OT) prophet Haggai: "For thus says the LORD of hosts: Once again, in a little while, I will shake the heavens and the earth and the sea and the dry land" (Hag 2:6, NRSVue). The "once again" refers to an undocumented event of the Israelites at Mount Sinai (Horeb). The earthquake reported by Haggai alludes to something that did not occur at Sinai (Horeb) in Exodus (19:1—24:18) but is reported elsewhere as if it had (Judg 5:4; Pss 68:8; 77:18; 114:7), because an earthquake is one of the elements in most theophanies. The message that the author of Hebrews conveys is that the final earthquake will be more encompassing than the supposed first; the final earthquake will remove what was created. What was created was associated with the realm of the finite; what will remain is the realm of the infinite. The dichotomy results in things unshaken—heaven—remaining. The author identifies unshaken things as God's kingdom, a stable, spiritual entity. Thus, readers should heed the voice of the one warning from heaven, unlike those who did not heed the voice of the one warning from the earth.

Heeding the warning from heaven results in showing gratitude to God by offering acceptable worship with reverence and awe. Gratitude is a response that the author of Hebrews wants to evoke from his readers, because he believes the unshakeable kingdom is present. Like Jesus, who demonstrated reverence (Heb 5:7), worshipers should approach God in awe. After all, according to the HB (OT) book of Deuteronomy, "the LORD . . . God is a devouring fire, a jealous God" (Deut 4:24, NRSVue). Throughout the Bible, God manifests his presence with fire; Hebrews' consuming fire implies judgment and punishment (Isa 33:14; Wis 16:16; Matt 25:41; 2 Thess 1:8; 1 Cor 3:13, 15; Heb 6:8; 2 Pet 3:7) once all created things are shaken by earthquake.

Psalm Response: "O God! Your way is holy! / No god is great like God! / You're the God who makes things happen; / you showed everyone what you can do— / Ocean saw you in action, God, / saw you and trembled with fear; / Deep Ocean was scared to death. / Clouds belched buckets of rain, / Sky exploded with thunder, / your arrows flashing this way and that. / From Whirlwind came your thundering voice, / Lightning expose the world, / Earth reeled and rocked. / You strode right through Ocean, / walked straight through roaring Ocean, / but nobody saw you come or go." (Ps 77:13-14, 16-19, TM)

Journal/Meditation: Does heeding a warning spark gratitude in you? Explain. What is your response to the author of Hebrews' words about created things being removed?

Summary

In this chapter about creation in the beginning, we explored biblical authors' perspectives before there was a beginning. In two different stories in the HB (OT) book of Genesis, the first being the younger of the two, the priestly writers explain a seven-day week with an emphasis on the last day (Saturday) being one of rest. In the second account of creation, being the older of the two, we went to the desert needing water for the garden. The HB (OT) book of Proverbs along with the OT (A) book of Wisdom declare that God created (Lady) Wisdom before anything else. The prophet Isaiah presents Yahweh (LORD) creating heavens and earth, like one would pitch a tent. After recounting the first story of creation, the author of the OT (A) book of Second Esdras adds several new twists to the existing stories of creation.

In the CB (NT), the author of Mark's Gospel presents Jesus looking at the suffering imposed by the Romans, when they destroyed Jerusalem in 70 CE; according to the Markan Jesus, there has been nothing like it since the creation of the world. The author of Hebrews states that created things will be removed to make way for uncreated things. Thus, whatever was created will be destroyed with an earthquake. And such is the variety of creation accounts in the Bible. All of their plurality invites deep reflection that does not result in reducing them to a singular account!

Biblical *C*reation Stories

2

Image of God

HUMANS

Scripture: "... God said, 'Let us make humans in our image, according to our likeness, and let them have dominion over the fish of the sea and over the birds of the air and over the cattle and over all the wild animals of the earth and over every creeping thing that creeps upon the earth.' So God created humans in his image, / in the image of God he created them, / male and female he created them." (Gen 1:26–27, NRSVue)

Reflection: As noted above in chapter 1, the seven-day narrative about the origin of the world is the younger of two different versions of creation. Humans are created on day six. In the story, God speaks about himself in the plural—us, our. In the world of the scribe who composed this account either right before or right after the end of the Babylonian Captivity of the Jews and their return to Jerusalem, a common feature of a kingdom was the king with his court or assembly of advisors. If kings had courts and advisors, then, certainly, God, king of Israel, had a court and an assembly of divine advisors. God creates humans after consultation with the assembly; thus, us, our. The word translated into English as humans by the NRSVue—previously translated as humankind by the NRSV—is the Hebrew word *adam*, which, when translated in the singular becomes *Adam*, even though it only means *man*.

The male and female are created in the image of God; that does not mean that they look like God, the way that people often speak about children looking like one or both of their parents! Being created in the image of God means that they are like God, who has dominion or rule over the whole world; he gives them dominion or rule over every living thing on the earth (Gen 1:28). In TM, Peterson captures the basic message of the passage, writing: "God spoke: 'Let us make human beings in our image, make them reflecting our nature . . . .' God created human beings; / he created them godlike, / Reflecting God's nature. / He created them male and female" (Gen 1:26a, 27, TM). *Nature* refers to the intrinsic or essential character of the man and woman; they are like God. Genesis 1:26–27 is echoed a few chapters later in Genesis 5:1b–2 in the narrative introducing Adam's descendants: "When God created humans, he made them in the likeness of God. Male and female he created them, and he blessed them and called them humans when they were created" (NRSVue). Like its counterpart above, the NRSV's *humankind* has been replaced by the NRSVue's *humans*; again, the Hebrew word is *adam* (man). Genesis 1:26–27 is also echoed in the HB (OT) book of Deuteronomy. While encouraging the Israelites to reflect upon their God-chosen status after escaping Egyptian slavery, Moses urges them to "ask . . . about former ages, long before [their] own, ever since the day that God created human beings on the earth . . ." (Deut 4:32, NRSVue).

Psalm Response: "GOD, brilliant Lord, / your name echoes around the world. . . . / I look at my micro-self and wonder, / Why do you bother with us? / Why take a second look our way? / Yet we've so narrowly missed being gods, / bright with Eden's dawn light. / You put us in charge of your handcrafted world, / repeated to us your Genesis-charge, / Made us lords . . . ." (Ps 8:9, 4–6a, TM)

Journal/Meditation: If you were a scribe rewriting the Scripture passage above for people today, how would you phrase it? What modern words would you use for *image* and *nature*?

GROUND

Scripture: ". . . [T]he LORD God formed man from the dust of the ground and breathed into his nostrils the breath of life, and the man became a living being. The LORD God took the man and put him in the garden of Eden to till it and keep it. . . . [T]he LORD God caused a deep sleep to fall upon the man, and he slept; then he took one of his ribs and closed up its place with flesh. And the rib that the LORD God had taken from the man he made into a woman and brought her to the man. Then the man said, / 'This at last is bone of my bones / and flesh of my flesh; / this one shall be called Woman, / for out of Man this one was taken.'" (Gen 2:7, 15, 21–23, NRSVue)

Reflection: The above account of the creation of man and woman is older than the first one in the HB (OT) book of Genesis. It features the LORD—Yahweh—creating the man (Hebrew, *adam*) from the soil (Hebrew, *adamah*), like a potter spins a wheel with clay and shapes the mud into whatever he or she wants it to be. The one difference is that the LORD breathes life into his creation. The Hebrew word *ruah* can be translated into English as breath, wind, or spirit. NRSVue, like its predecessor, NRSV, prefers to translate it as *breath*. That is because for ancient people breathing characterized life; living beings (people) breathed; dead people did not breath. A better biblical translation would be *spirit*; the LORD inspirited the mud-man. The man's spirit shares in Yahweh's Spirit. Today, in addition to the vital sign of respiration, medical personnel also check body temperature, pulse rate, and blood pressure, not to mention brain waves for signs of life.

There can be little doubt that this older account of the creation of man and woman emerges from a patriarchal society. The woman is created from one of the man's ribs; she is a secondary creation, reflecting the patriarchal presupposition that a man owns his wife, while a father with a daughter sells her to a prospective husband. According to this older account of the creation of woman, she is, literally, a rib bone of the man's bones, mud-flesh of his flesh. Even her name Woman (in Hebrew, *ishshah*) reflects her origin, Man (in Hebrew, *ish*). She is given to the man as a helper (Gen 2:18) to till the garden and keep it (Gen 2:15). No breath of life is breathed into her; she is not considered to be a living being! Deutero-Isaiah (chapters 40 through 55) records the LORD stating, "I made the earth / and created humankind upon it" (Isa 45:12a, NRSVue). While condemning the king of Tyre, the prophet Ezekiel, tells him that he was "in Eden, the garden of God" (Ezek 28:13, NRSVue), where he was "blameless in [his] ways / from the day that [he was] created" (Ezek 15:28ab, NRSVue) until he entered corrupt trade practices.

Psalm Response: "[GOD, i]s there anyplace I can go to avoid your Spirit? / to be out of your sight? / Oh yes, you shaped me first inside, then out; / you formed me in my mother's womb, / I thank you, High God—you're breathtaking! / You know me inside and out, / you know every bone in my body; / You know exactly how I was made, bit by bit, / how I was sculpted from nothing into something." (Ps 139:7, 13, 15 TM)

Journal/Meditation: If you were a scribe rewriting the Scripture passage above for people today, how would you phrase it? Be sure to use *human*, remembering that human comes from *humus*, meaning earth.

IMAGE OF ETERNITY

Scripture: ". . . God created us for incorruption / and made us in the image of his own eternity . . . . (Wis 2:23, NRSVue)

Reflection: The author of the OT (A) book of Wisdom states that because some people "did not know the secret purposes of God" (Wis 2:22, NRSVue), they were led astray. The secret plan, according to the author, is that people were created to be immortal, like God's eternity. The author of Wisdom has interpreted Genesis' "image of God" (Gen 1:27, NRSVue) to include immortality for God's human creation. Humankind was created to be immortal because God breathed—inspirited—people, divinized them, gave them eternal life, according to the Johannine Jesus (John 3:15, 16, 36; 4:14, 36; 5:24, 39; 6:27, 40, 47, 54, 60; 10:28; 12:25, 50; 17:2, 3). "Wisdom protected the first-formed father of the world," (Adam) according to Wisdom, "when he alone had been created . . ." (Wis 10:1ab, NRSVue). This is because, according to the OT (A) book of Sirach, wisdom "is created with the faithful in the womb" (Sir 1:14b, NRSVue). After all, the Lord "created humans in the beginning, / and he left them in the power of their own inclinations" (Sir 15:14, NRSVue). NRSV, echoing the garden of Eden story in Genesis, states that the Lord left them "in the power of their own free choice" (Sir 15:14, NRSV).

Later in Sirach, the author clarifies: "All humans come from the ground, and humankind was created out of dust" (Sir 33:10, NRSVue): "The Lord created humans out of earth / and makes them return to it again" (Sir 17:1, NRSVue). The Hebrew word translated into English as humankind is *adam* (man), echoing the older Genesis creation account, because "above every other created living being was Adam" (Sir 49:16, NRSVue), the man made from dust (dirt, clay) by the potter God. Keeping in mind that God placed the man in the garden to till and keep it, Sirach reflects that "hard labor . . . was created by the Most High" (Sir 7:15, NRSVue). Echoing the Genesis story about Adam being placed in the garden of Eden to till it and keep it, the author of the OT (A) book of Sirch declares: "Hard work was created for everyone, / and a heavy yoke is laid on the children of Adam, / from the day they come forth from their mother's womb / until the day they return to the mother of all the living"—earth, soil, dust, dirt (Sir 40:1, NRSVue). Because humankind was created from the ground, "[p]ride was not created for human beings" (Sir 10:18, NRSVue), even though they are made in the image of God's eternity.

Psalm Response: "Your love, GOD, is my song, and I'll sing it! / I'm forever telling everyone how faithful you are. / I'll never quit telling the story of your love— / how you built the cosmos / and guaranteed everything in it. / Your love has always been our lives' / foundation, / your fidelity has been the roof over our world. / You own the cosmos—you made everything in it . . . . / Remember my sorrow and how short life is. / Did you create men and women for nothing but this? / We'll see death soon enough. Everyone does. / So where is the love you're so famous for, Lord?" (Ps 89:1–2, 11a, 46–49, TM)

Journal/Meditation: Without using the word soul, of what composition do you consider yourself to be? What is God's purpose for you?

FROM CREATION TO REDEMPTION

Scripture: ". . . [T]hus says the LORD, / he who created you, O Jacob, / he who formed you, O Israel: / Do not fear, for I have redeemed you; / I have called you by name; you are mine." (Isa 43:1, NRSVue)

Reflection: The above passage from Deutero-Isaiah is called a salvation oracle by biblical scholars. The divine speech recorded by the second prophet Isaiah is the result of a process of theological reflection. The LORD declares that he has created the people of Judah (Jacob) and Israel; this means that he owns them, like a master owns slaves. They have nothing to fear because his claim to mastery or control is also his assurance of protection. Furthermore, he has called them by name; he has given them authority and responsibility—"everyone who is called by [his] name, / whom [he] created for [his] glory, / whom [he] formed and made" (Isa 43:7, NRSVue). As the LORD lays claim to whom he has created, he also redeems, ransoms, buys back, like a master buys back a slave he previously sold. Redeeming means that God is doing something new; he is bestowing the gift of freedom. Understood in the context that Deutero-Isaiah was written at the end of the Babylonian exile, the redemption is the freedom of the people to return from exile. Their Creator is claiming what he owns.

The OT (A) Second Book of Esdras presents the man (Adam) as the ancestor of all Israel—Jacob and Israel. ". . . [F]rom him we have all come, the people whom you [, O Lord,] have chosen" (2 Esd 6:54, NRSVue), says Ezra. This leads Ezra to conclude that it was for the Jews (Israelites, Hebrews) that God created the world (2 Esd 6:55, 59), although that it is not a biblical idea. After being instructed by the angel Uriel, God in disguise, Ezra concludes that evil has infiltrated "almost all who have been created" and brought humankind "into corruption and the ways of death" (2 Esd 7:48, NRSVue). Upon his realization that only a few will be saved—in contrast to what Isaiah says—Ezra cries, "O earth, what have you brought forth, if the mind is made out of the dust like the other created things?" (2 Esd 7:62, NRSVue) Then, Ezra appeals to God's mercy; the Most High is called "the judge because if he did not pardon those who were created by his word and blot out the multitude of their sins, there would probably be left only very few of the innumerable multitude" (2 Esd 7:139–40, NRSVue). God answers: "The Most High made this world for the sake of many but the world to come for the sake of only a few. Many have been created, but only a few shall be saved." (2 Esd 8:1, 3, NRSVue). Ezra is not yet finished. He tells the Lord: ". . . [Y]ou alone exist, and we are a work of your hands, as you have declared. And because you give life to the body that is now fashioned in the womb and furnish it with members, what you have created is preserved amid fire and water, and for nine months the womb endures your creature that has been created in it. But that which keeps and that which is kept shall both be kept by your keeping. And when the womb gives up again what has been created in it, you have commanded that from the members themselves (that is, from the breasts) milk, the fruit of the breasts, should be supplied, so that what has been fashioned may be nourished for a time, and afterward you will still guide it in your mercy" (2 Esd 8:7–11, NRSVue). Finally, Ezra must conclude: "[T]he Most High did not intend that anyone should be destroyed, but those who were created have themselves defiled the name of him who made them and have been ungrateful to him who repaired life for them now" (2 Esd 8:59b–60, NRSVue). In other words, ". . . [T]hose who have been created in this world . . . have become corrupt in their ways" (2 Esd 9:19, NRSVue). In the CB (NT), the Matthean Jesus says the same thing: ". . . [M]any are called, but few are chosen" (Matt 21:14, NRSVue).

Psalm Response: "Soak me in your laundry [, God,] and I'll come out clean, / scrub me and I'll have a snow-white life. / Don't look too close for blemishes, / give me a clean bill of health. / God, make a fresh start in me, / shape a Genesis week from the chaos of my life. / Don't throw me out with the trash, / or fail to breathe holiness in me. / Bring me back from gray exile, / put a fresh wind in my sails! / Commute my death sentence, God, my salvation God, / and I'll sing anthems to your life-giving ways." (Ps 51:7, 9–12, 14, TM)

Journal/Meditation: For whom do you think the world exists? Explain. Do you agree or disagree with Ezra's conclusion as for whom the world exists? Explain. Do you think all people will be redeemed or only a few? Explain.

WOMAN CAME FROM MAN

Scripture: "... [A] man ought not to have his head veiled, since he is the image and reflection of God, but woman is the reflection of man. Indeed, man was not made from woman but woman from man. Neither was man created for the sake of woman but woman for the sake of man. Nevertheless, in the Lord woman is not independent of man or man independent of woman. For just as woman came from man, so man comes through woman, but all things come from God." (1 Cor 11:7–9, 11–12, NRSVue)

Reflection: The basic issue of chapter 11 of Paul's First Letter to the Corinthians concerns women at worship, specifically whether they cover their heads or not! Being Jewish, Paul knows that during worship men do not cover their heads, and women, who may not appear in public without a head covering, are to have their heads covered. Other than appealing only to custom, Paul reinterprets the creation of man and woman accounts in the HB (OT) book of Genesis. A man does not cover his head because he is created in the image of God (Gen 1:27), even though the text of the first account of creation states, "God created humans in his image, / in the image of God he created them, / male and female he created them" (Gen 1:27, NRSVue). Thus, both man and woman are in the image of God and both reflect the divine. But that will not advance Paul's position!

The text of the second account of creation states, "... [T]he LORD God formed man from the dust of the ground and breathed into his nostrils the breath of life, and the man became a living being" (Gen 2:7, NRSVue). Then, later, "... [T]he LORD God caused a deep sleep to fall upon the man, and he slept; then he took one of his ribs and closed up its place with flesh. And the rib that the LORD God had taken from the man he made into a woman ..." (Gen 2:21–22, NRSV). From all appearances, it looks like Paul has melded the two accounts of creation into one, making man the image and reflection of God and the woman the reflection of man. Having in mind the second account of creation, Paul declares that man was not made from woman, but woman was made from man. Likewise, again having the second story of creation in mind, Paul states that man was not created for the sake of woman, but woman was created as a helpmate for man. Then, in the *nevertheless* clause, Paul has in mind the first account of creation insofar as woman is not independent of man or man independent of woman; they are created together equally. While in the second account of creation, woman came from—was created from a rib—man, so, when it comes to conceiving and giving birth, man comes through woman. However, in both accounts of creation, all things come from God. Thus, according to Paul, a woman covers her head during worship not just because it is a custom, but because it reflects the order of creation.

Psalm Response: "Thank GOD! He deserves your thanks. / *His love never quits*. / Thank the God of all gods, / *His love never quits*. Thank the Lord of all lords. / *His love never quits*. / Thank the miracle-working God, / *His love never quits*. / The God whose skill formed the cosmos, / *His love never quits*. / The God who laid out earth on ocean foundations, / *His love never quits*. / The God who filled the skies with light, / *His love never quits*. / The sun to watch over the day, *His love never quits*. / Moon and stars as guardians of the night, / *His love never quits*. / Takes care of everyone in time of need. / *His love never quits*. / Thank God, who did it all! / *His love never quits*." (Ps 136:1–9, 23, 26, TM)

Journal/Meditation: What is your immediate response to Paul's words about man being the image and reflection of God and woman being the image and reflection of man? What do you think about Paul's answer to the question: Should women cover their heads during worship? What do you think about the reasons he gives for his answer?

Summary:

The plurality of chapter 1's In the Beginning, continues in the plurality of chapter 2's Image of God. In the first (younger) account, man and woman are created in God's image. In the second (older) account, man is inspirited with life, and woman receives her life by being created from one of man's ribs! The OT (A) book of Wisdom states that people were created in the image of God's eternity, that is, they were created to be immortal. This idea is derived from the ambiguity of the Hebrew word *ruah*, which can mean breath, spirit, or wind. Thus, people are immortal because God inspirited them; he divinized them when he breathed the breath of life into them. In the texts about the creation of people, a tension is established between people created from mud, soil, dirt, and created to be eternal, immortal, divine. The tension is never resolved. The LORD redeems, ransoms, buys back what he has inspirited or divinized. In other words, the Creator claims what he owns, what he created. Many are called, but few are chosen, according to the Matthean Jesus. And with Paul's reinterpretation of the dual creation accounts of man and woman, the reader is back to where he or she began: two different stories of creation in the HB (OT) book of Genesis. The truth concerning the creation of man and woman is, indeed, plural.

Biblical *Creation* Stories

3

Creator of All

WHOLE UNIVERSE

Scripture: "He who lives forever created the whole universe." (Sir 18:1, NRSVue)

Reflection: The author of the OT (A) book of Sirach does not need to state that God created the whole universe; he only needs to say that the one who lives forever did it. Every reader knows that the Lord (Yahweh) lives forever. The author of the OT (A) book of Wisdom adds that God "created the world out of formless matter" (Wis 11:17, NRSVue). While other gods create new things from existing things, the Lord creates (forms) new things from matter that has no form. Later in the book, the author reflects on the beauty of all created things, urging his readers to "know how much better than these is their Lord, / for the author of beauty created them" (Wis 13:3bc, NRSVue). Then, the author concludes, "For from the greatness and beauty of created things / comes a corresponding perception of their Creator" (Wis 13:5, NRSVue). In other words, if one wants to know something about God, all he or she must do is to be aware of what exists and reflect upon its beauty!

Other biblical authors specify what the Lord created in the whole universe. For example, in a prayer found in the OT (A) book of Judith, "the

Lord God" is blessed and identified as he "who created the heavens and the earth" (Jdt 13:18, NRSVue). Likewise, in the OT (A) book Bel and the Dragon, Daniel, a companion of the Persian King Cyrus, declares that "the living God . . . created heaven and earth" (Bel 1:5, NRSVue [Dan 14:5]). The First Book of Esdras in the OT (A) records a letter sent to King Darius reporting that the elders of the Jews who had returned from Babylonian exile identified themselves as "the servants of the Lord who created the heaven and the earth" (1 Esd 6:12, NRSVue), while the OT (A) Third Book of Maccabees records the prayer of the high priest Simon identifying God as the King who "created the boundless and immeasurable earth" (3 Macc 2:9, NRSVue). In the CB (NT), the author of Revelation observes an angel swearing "by him who lives forever and ever, / who created heaven and what is in it [and] the earth and what is in it" (Rev 10:6, NRSVue).

Psalm Response: "[GOD, y]ou own the cosmos—you made everything in it, / everything from atom to archangel. / You positioned the North and South Poles; / the mountains . . . sing duets to you. / With your well-muscled arm and your grip of steel— / nobody trifles with you!" (Ps 89:11–13, TM)

Journal/Meditation: What do you think creation out of formless matter means? What are its implications? Consequences? What specific thing reflects the beauty of the Creator to you?

ALL CREATURES AND PEOPLE

Scripture: "I will sing to my God a new song; / O Lord, you are great and glorious, / wonderful in strength, invincible. / Let all your creatures serve you, / for you spoke, and they were made. / You sent forth your spirit, and it formed them; / there is none that can resist your voice." (Jdt 16:13–14, NRSVue)

Reflection: The OT (A) book of Judith ends with a hymn of praise, from which the above verses are taken. This victory song, which was most likely composed and added to the end of the book after the unknown author had finished the novella, celebrates the heroine's defeat of her enemy by cutting off his head with his own sword in his own tent! Judith's hymn of praise or victory song shares motifs with the psalms. First, the author states that it is a new song, like Psalms 33:3; 96:1; 144:9; and 149:1. Second, it shares verses with Psalm 33; Judith 16:13 is like Psalm 33:3; Judith 16:14a is like Psalm 33:9; Judith 16:14b is like Psalm 33:6; and Judith 16:14c is like Psalm 33:8. Third, Judith 16:14b also resembles Psalm 104:30a: "When you [, LORD,] send forth your spirit, [creatures] are created . . ." (Ps 104:30a, NRSVue).

Here it is important to note that the Hebrew word *ruah* can be translated into English as *spirit, breath,* or *wind*. Some English Bibles translate the verse in Judith using the word *breath*, echoing the HB (OT) book of Genesis' mention that God "breathed into [the man's] nostrils the breath of life, and the man became a living being" (Gen 2:7, NRSVue).

Because the common Hebrew Bible understanding was that God created everything and everyone—all creatures—the prophet Malachi reinterpreted that presupposition using the metaphor of *father*. He put it in question form: "Have we not all one father?" (Mal 2:10a, NRSVue) Underlying the metaphor is the patriarchal, biological understanding that just as a man creates offspring (and various physical things), God creates everything. That's why Malachi's second question is this: "Has not one God created us?" (Mal 2:10b, NRSVue) The prophet presumes that his readers will answer both questions with a "Yes."

Psalm Response: "Hallelujah! / Praise GOD from heaven, / praise him from the mountaintops; / Praise him, sun and moon, / praise him, you morning stars; / Praise him, high heaven, / praise him, heavenly rain clouds; / Praise, oh let them praise the name of GOD— / he spoke the word, and there they were! / He set them in place / from all time to eternity; / He gave his orders, / and that's it!" (Ps 148:1, 3–6, TM)

Journal/Meditation: What new song can you sing in praise of God today? Critique the prophet Malachi's metaphor of *father* for God from a modern understanding of biology. What do you discover?

ALL THINGS

Scripture: "Although I [, Paul,] am the very least of all the saints, this grace [of God] was given to me to bring to the gentiles the news of the boundless riches of Christ and to make everyone see what is the plan of the mystery hidden for ages in God, who created all things . . . ." (Eph 3:8–9, NRSVue)

Reflection: Because what is known today as Christianity grew out of Judaism, the biblical reader should expect to find Jewish presuppositions in the Christian Bible (New Testament). Such is the case in the second-generation Pauline Letter to the Ephesians; biblical scholars do not think that the historical Paul wrote the Letter to the Ephesians, but one of his disciples did to adapt his gospel for a new generation of gentile believers. Whoever the author of the letter is, he presupposes the HB (OT) understanding that God created all things. The author of Ephesians presents Paul's mission—gracing—to make Christ known to the gentiles; he wants all to see—understand—that God's plan, hidden for ages, is being revealed. The author of the letter interprets the hidden plan of God, who created all things, to be that the "gentiles have become fellow heirs, members of the same body, and sharers in the promise in Christ Jesus through the gospel" (Eph 3:6, NRSVue). For the gentiles, non-Jews, this is, indeed, good news (gospel). However, for the Jews, who thought of themselves as God's chosen people, this is bad news! Nevertheless, the author of this letter understands that God has created one new humanity in place of the two (Jews and Gentiles) through Jesus' cross (Eph 2:14–16).

A similar idea is found in the second-generation Pauline Letter to the Colossians. Employing the concept of wisdom being created first and present as God's advisor during creation, the author of Colossians states that Jesus Christ is the visible "image of the invisible God, the firstborn of all creation" (Col 1:15, NRSVue). Furthermore, "all things in heaven and on earth were created, things visible and invisible, . . . through him and for him" (Col 1:16, NRSVue). The author continues: "He himself is before all things, and in him all things hold together" (Col 1:17, NRSVue). Thus, all things remain in their created existence through and for Christ, the agent of creation. God is the creator, but Christ is the agent of creation. According to the author of the letter, Christ is the final goal of creation. He has "first place in everything" (Col 1:18, NRSVue), and "in him the fullness of God was pleased to dwell" (Col 1:19, NRSVue). Through Christ, "God was pleased to reconcile to himself all things, whether on earth or in heaven, by making peace through the blood of his cross" (Col 1:20, NRSVue). In other words, the Creator of all things through Christ brought all created things (back) together through him. Such is the gospel "proclaimed to every creature under heaven" (Col 1:23, NRSVue) by this second-generation Pauline author.

Canticle Response: "Holy, holy, holy / Is God our Master, Sovereign-Strong, / THE WAS, THE IS, THE COMING. / Worthy, O Master! Yes, our God! / Take the glory! the honor! the power! / You created it all; / It was created because you wanted it." (Rev 4:8b, 11, TM)

Journal/Meditation: What are your presuppositions about the creation of all things? Be specific.

SPECIFIC THINGS

Scripture: ". . . [T]he one who forms the mountains, creates the wind, / reveals his thoughts to mortals, / makes the morning darkness, / and treads on the heights of the earth— / the LORD, the God of hosts, is his name!" (Amos 4:13)

Reflection: Other than attributing the creation of all things—humans and creatures—to God, various HB (OT) authors attribute the creation of specific things to God. For example, the HB (OT) prophet Amos names the LORD God as the creator of mountains, wind, and dawn. While Amos states that God reveals his thoughts to people, he doesn't explain how that is accomplished. Following in the HB (OT) presupposition that the universe is made of three levels, above the middle—earth—are the heavens, where God walks, the OT (A) book of Sirach presents a list of things God has "created for vengeance" (Sir 39:28–29, NRSVue); among those are winds, which can dislodge mountains (Sir 39:28), along with fire, hail, famine, and pestilence (Sir 39:29). While that list might create conflict in modern ears, the presupposition of the author of the book is this: "Good things and bad, life and death, / poverty and wealth, come from the Lord" (Sir 11:14, NRSVue). The author of the OT (A) book of Second Esdras disagrees: "I set aside evil and created good, for I am the Living One, says the Lord" (2 Esd 2:14). In the CB (NT) the author of First Timothy agrees: "... [E]verything created by God is good..." (1 Tim 4:4, NRSVue).

In one of his lengthy prayers, Ezra reminds the Most High of what he created: "O sovereign Lord, from every forest of the earth, and from all its trees you have chosen one vine, and from all the lands of the world you have chosen for yourself one region, and from all the flowers of the world you have chosen for yourself one lily, and from all the depths of the sea you have filled for yourself one river, and from all the cities that have been built you have consecrated Zion for yourself, and from all the birds that have been created you have named for yourself one dove, and from all the flocks that have been made you have provided for yourself one sheep, and from all the multitude of people you have gotten for yourself one people, and to this people, whom you have loved, you have given the law that is approved by all" (2 Esd 5:23–27, NRSVue; [4 Esd 5:23–27]). In Ezra's prayer, the one vine is a recurring biblical image for Israel (Ps 80:8–16; Isa 5:7; Jer 2:21; Ezek 17:6; Hos 10:1, 14:7; Joel 1:7). The one region, the land of Israel, is promised (Gen 12:1). In biblical literature, the lily is premier among flowers (1 Kgs 7:19, 22, 26; 2 Chr 4:5; Song 2:1–2; Hos 14:5; Sir 39:14) and Israel is likened to a lily (Hos 14:5). The one river in Ezra's prayer is the Jordan, since it is the most prominent river in Israel, and the city (code name Zion) is Jerusalem, "bound firmly together" (Ps 122:3, NRSVue). The author allegorically interprets Song 2:14; 5:2 as applying to Israel, a dove. Because God is presented as the shepherd often in biblical literature, the people of

Israel are the sheep (Pss 23:1–6, 74:1, 79:13, 80:1, 95:7; Hos 4:16; Mic 7:14). The one people in Ezra's prayer refers to the election of Israel—an idea basic to biblical thought. Finally, while Torah (law) may be regarded by all people, it was given to Israel.

Not to be ignored in this biblical list of specific things God created are physicians (Sir 38:1, 12), medicines (Sir 38:4), and "certain foods, which God created to be received with thanksgiving by those who believe and know the truth" (1 Tim 4:3).

Psalm Response: "Listen, Shepherd, Israel's Shepherd— / get all your . . . sheep together. / Remember how you brought a young vine from Egypt, / cleared out the brambles and briers / and planted your very own vineyard? / You prepared the good earth, / you planted her roots deep; / the vineyard filled the land. / Your vine soared high and shaded the mountains, / even dwarfing the giant cedars. / Your vine ranged west to the Sea, / east to the River. / God-of-the-Angel-armies, turn our way! / Take a good look at what's happened / and attend to this vine. / Care for what you once tenderly planted— / the vine you raised from a shoot." (Ps 80:1, 8–11, 14–15, TM)

Journal/Meditation: Specifically, what created things do you attribute directly to God? Explain.

Summary:

God—identified as the one who lives forever—created heaven and earth, all things, the universe out of formless matter. In this chapter, we have reflected on the beauty of created things, because it leads to the perception of the Creator. Using the first Genesis creation account, many biblical authors presume that God spoke and things sprang into existence. Speaking of God metaphorically as a father, the Christian Bible (New Testament) declares that God created through Jesus Christ. A new humanity was formed from two—Jews and Gentiles—along with all created things: mountains, wind, dawn, fire, hail, famine, pestilence, life, death, poverty, wealth, etc. God created both good things and bad things—that is another biblical way of stating that the LORD created all things.

Biblical
*C*reation
Stories

4

Creation Destroyed

BY FLOOD

Scripture: "The LORD saw that the wickedness of humans was great in the earth and that every inclination of the thoughts of their hearts was only evil continually. And the LORD was sorry that he had made humans on the earth, and it grieved him to his heart. So the LORD said, 'I will blot out from the earth the humans I have created—people together with animals and creeping things and birds of the air—for I am sorry that I have made them.'" (Gen 6:5–7, NRSVue)

Reflection: The biblical authors wrote about God creating the heavens and everything therein and the earth and everything on it; they concluded that if God could create, he could also destroy what he created. Thus, the authors of the HB (OT) book of Genesis conclude that the transgression of the man and woman in the garden, the killing of Abel by his brother Cain, and other such behavior leads to an awareness that humans are wicked. The narrator states that their hearts were inclined to choose evil continually. Since the biblical heart is where intellect—knowing right and wrong—and the will—wanting to do right or wrong—come together, God concludes that people have been willing to do more bad than good. Such divine knowledge grieves the LORD's heart, and he regrets having created them. His regret results in a plan to remove them from the earth, along with everything else he has created. The means for their removal will not be outright extermination, but the employment of a flood, a story well known in Babylon, situated between the Tigris and Euphrates rivers.

In a similar vein, the author of the OT (A) book of Sirach reflects upon the wretchedness of humankind in chapter 40. People are plagued by perplexities, fear, anxieties, death, bloodshed, and strife, not to mention calamities, famine, ruin, and plague (Sir 40:1–9). According to Sirach, "All these were created for the lawless, / and on their account the flood came" (Sir 40:10, NRSVue). While human misery abounds for all, the author is convinced that sinners receive seven times more strife than the godly—like Noah (Gen 6:8), a righteous man (Gen 7:1).

Psalm Response: "Bravo, GOD, bravo! / Gods and all angels shout, 'Encore!' / In awe before the glory, / in awe before God's visible power. / Stand at attention! . . . . / GOD thunders across the waters; / Brilliant, his voice and his face, streaming brightness— / GOD across the flood waters. / GOD's thunder tympanic, / GOD's thunder symphonic. / GOD's thunder smashes cedars, / GOD topples the northern cedars. / The mountain ranges skip like spring colts, / The high ridges jump like wild kid goats. / GOD's thunder spits fire; / GOD thunders, the wilderness quakes; / He makes the desert . . . shake. / GOD's thunder sets the oak trees dancing / A wild dance, whirling; the pelting rain strips their branches, / We fall to our knees—we call out, 'Glory!' / Above the floodwaters is GOD's throne / from which his power flows, / from which he rules the world." (Ps 29:1–10, TM)

Journal/Meditation: Do you think humans are wicked by nature? Explain. Why do you think bad things happen to people? Explain.

ABOMINABLE CREATION

Scripture: ". . . [T]here will be a visitation . . . upon the idols of the nations, / because, though part of what God created, they became an abomination, / stumbling blocks for human souls / and a trap for the feet of the foolish." (Wis 14:11, NRSVue)

Reflection: The author of the OT (A) book of Wisdom addresses the worship of creation rather than the worship of the Creator in chapters 13 through 15. He begins by lamenting that people are ignorant of God; they are not able to conclude from the good things that exist that there is one who exists, nor recognize the artisan while noticing his works (Wis 13:1). The author of beauty created beautiful things. In other words, the beauty of the created world reflects the intelligent mind of the Creator. After establishing his premise, the author of Wisdom applies it to the wood used to create a ship (Wis 13:10—14:7) and the wood used to create an idol (Wis 14:8—15:19). The wood used in shipbuilding is a gift of the Creator of the world. This leads the author to remember Noah, when "the hope of the world took refuge on a raft . . . guided by [God's] hand" (Wis 14:6, NRSVue). ". . . [B]lessed is the wood by which righteousness comes" (Wis 14:7, NRSVue).

However, because ancient ships usually carried a carved-from-wood idol on the bow, today known as a figurehead, the author concludes that the good wood—able to reflect the Creator—was abused when it was used to create a bad idol, in whom people onboard place their trust! The blessedness of wood (Wis 14:7) becomes accursed (Wis 14:8), because divine judgment will fall upon the idol made from it and the person who made it (Wis 14:9). God's judgment (visitation) falls upon all who engage in idolatry. In other words, trees, wood, and wooden things are good, but wooden idols, even though they are part of what God created (trees, wood), are abominations; they cause people to fall into false worship.

Psalm Response: "Praise GOD from earth, . . . / Fire and hail, snow and ice, / hurricanes obeying his orders; / Mountains and all hills, / apple orchards and cedar forests; / Wild beasts and herds of cattle, / snakes, and birds in flight; / Earth's kings and all races, / leaders and important people, / Robust men and women in their prime, / and yes, graybeards and little children. / Let them praise the name of GOD— / it's the only Name worth praising. / His radiance exceeds anything in earth and sky . . . ." (Ps 148:7–13, TM)

Journal/Meditation: Identify three things God created and how they are not used as they were intended. Where do you see the worship of creation rather than worship of the Creator occurring?

SOMETHING NEW

Scripture: ". . . [T]he LORD spoke to Moses: 'Speak to the congregation saying: Get away from the dwellings of Korah, Dathan, and Abiram.' So Moses got up and went to Dathan and Abiram; the elders of Israel followed him. He spoke to the congregation, saying, 'Turn away from the tents of these wicked men and touch nothing of theirs, or you will be swept away for all their sins.' So they got away from the dwellings of Korah, Dathan, and Abiram, and Dathan and Abiram came out and stood at the entrances of their tents, together with their wives, their children, and their little ones. And

Moses said, 'This is how you shall know that the LORD has sent me to do all these works; it has not been of my own accord: If these people die a natural death or if a natural fate comes to them, then the LORD has not sent me. But if the LORD creates something new, and the ground opens its mouth and swallows them up, with all that belongs to them, and they go down alive into Sheol, then you shall know that these men have despised the LORD.' As soon as he finished speaking all these words, the ground under them was split apart. The earth opened its mouth and swallowed them, along with their households—everyone who belonged to Korah and all their goods. So they with all that belonged to them went down alive into Sheol; the earth closed over them, and they perished from the midst of the assembly. (Num 16:23–33, NRSVue)

Reflection: The above biblical story is but a small part of a much longer narrative about a revolt by Korah, Dathan, and Abiram, along with 250 Israelite men, in the HB (OT) book of Numbers against Moses and Aaron. Those revolting do so because they think Moses and Aaron are exalting themselves above all other Israelites. Moses instructs them to put live coals in their censors—bowls—in which incense was burned and be prepared for the LORD's answer. The question raised is about who can legitimately perform the duties of the priest in offering incense and sacrifices at the central altar. Is only Aaron and his sons, with the help of Levites, permitted to perform those duties? Korah, a rebel leader, is from the tribe of Levi, but Dathan and Abiram are from the tribe of Rueben. Before the showdown is to take place, Moses tells the Israelites to get away from the tents of the rebels.

Then, the rebels with their families stand at the entrances of their tents. And Moses instructs all present how to interpret whatever takes place next. If those leading the revolt die natural deaths, the congregation is to conclude that the rebels are correct; the LORD did not call Moses to do the work he has been doing. However, if the LORD creates something new, then the assembly will know that the LORD holds the rebels in contempt. Just as Moses finishes giving his interpretative speech, the ground under the rebels and their families opens and they fall into the earth and the earth closes over them. Indeed, the LORD created something new. In a three-storied universe, the first level below the earth is Sheol; it is the place where the dead live. That is why this account states that they "went down alive into Sheol" (Num 16:33, NRSVue). The 250 men accompanying the rebellious leaders were consumed by the LORD's fire, while they were burning incense on fiery coals (Num 16:35).

Psalm Response: "After our parents left Egypt, / they took your wonders for granted, [GOD,] / forgot your great and wonderful love. / [GOD] saved them from a life of oppression, / pried them loose from the grip of the enemy. / But it wasn't long before they forgot the whole thing; / wouldn't wait to be told what to do. / They only cared about pleasing themselves in that desert, / provoked God with their insistent demands. / One day in camp some grew jealous of Moses, / also of Aaron, holy priest of GOD. / The ground opened and swallowed Dathan, / then buried Abiram's gang. / Fire flared against that rebel crew / and torched them to a cinder." (Ps 106:7, 10, 13, 16–18, TM)

Journal/Meditation: What new things have you witnessed the LORD create for you during your life? How were they destructive? Explain.

Summary

Biblically, if God (the LORD) can create, he can also destroy what he created. He destroys creation with a great flood in order to re-create or re-populate it. God is like a potter at the wheel taking his hand and collapsing the mud—because it is not in the form he desires—in order to reshape it into what he wants. Wooden idols are abominations, because they are made by people from God's creation of trees; people end up worshiping creation instead of worshiping the Creator. The LORD even creates something new in order to destroy some of his creation. The earth opens to swallow those who stage a revolt against Moses and Aaron. God uses the Assyrians' newly-acquired power to destroy the Kingdom of Israel (2 Kgs 17:1–41): ". . . [T]he LORD was very angry with Israel and removed them out of his sight; none was left but the tribe of Judah alone" (2 Kgs 17:18, NRSVue) and ". . . [T]he LORD removed Israel out of his sight, as he had foretold through all his servants the prophets. So Israel was exiled from their own land to Assyria until this day" (2 Kgs 17:23, NRSVue). The LORD also uses the newly-acquired power of the Babylonians, referred to by the prophet Ezekiel as God's sword. "I am coming against you [, land of Israel (Judah)] and will draw my sword out of its sheath . . . . A sword, a sword is sharpened; / it is also polished; / it is sharpened for slaughter, / honed to flash like lightning! . . . The word of the LORD came to me [, Ezekiel]: Mortal, mark out two roads for the sword of the king of Babylon to come . . ." (Ezek 21:3, 9–10, 18–19, NRSVue). Ezekiel is even told by the LORD to erect a signpost for the king of Babylon to find his way to Judah (Ezek 21:19–23). Such is the way that God creates something new in order to destroy some of his creation that, for whatever reason, he deems worthy of destruction!

Biblical *Creation* Stories

5

Something Old, Something New

CLOUD

Scripture: "... [T]he LORD will create over the whole site of Mount Zion and over its places of assembly a cloud by day and smoke and the shining of a flaming fire by night. Indeed, over all the glory there will be a canopy." (Isa 4:5, NRSVue)

Reflection: Keeping in mind that there are several prophets Isaiah collected into one biblical book over the years of transmission, oral and written, some biblical scholars think that Isaiah 4:2–5 was added after the experience of exile in Babylon and return to Jerusalem (Judah). Other biblical scholars think that the passage logically follows the judgment addressed by the prophet against Jerusalem (Judah) immediately before it (Isa 3:1—4:1). Thus, Isaiah 3:1—4:1 is not God's final word; God's purpose is to purify Jerusalem (Judah). No matter the position taken, the prophet declares that restoration will occur, and that restoration will involve the creation of something old and something new.

That something old is a cloud over Mount Zion, a literary code for Jerusalem and Judah. In the HB (OT) book of Exodus, a cloud is the sign of the divine presence. After the Hebrews escape from Egypt, they are led by the LORD as a cloud (Exod 13:21). Once they get to Mount Sinai (Horeb), the LORD tells Moses, "I am going to come to you in a dense cloud..." (Exod 19:9, NRSVue), and the narrator makes a point of writing, "On the morning of the third day there was... a thick cloud on the mountain..." (Exod 19:16, NRSVue). More specifically, the divine presence is signified by the "pillar of cloud by day... and... a pillar of fire by night..." (Exod 13:21, NRSVue). In the narrative about the LORD's descent upon Mount Sinai (Horeb), the author states that the mountain "was wrapped in smoke, because the LORD had descended upon it in fire..." (Exod 19:18, NRSVue).

The cloud, smoke, and fire—things old—are presented by the prophet Isaiah as things new. Over all the glory of the divine presence, there is a canopy; God's protecting presence will cover Zion (Jerusalem and Judah), in a way like the protection he gave by leading the Hebrews out of Egyptian slavery (Exod 13:21–22), through the Red Sea (Exod 14:24–25), and to Mount Sinai (Horeb) (Exod 19:1): "He spread a cloud for a covering" (Ps 105:39a, NRSVue). Furthermore, just like there was an exodus out of Egyptian slavery, there will be, according to Isaiah, an exodus out of Babylonian captivity. Something old becomes something new.

Psalm Response: "Listen, dear friends, to God's truth, / bend your ears to what I tell you. / I'm chewing on the morsel of a proverb; / I'll let you in on the sweet old truths, / Stories we heard from our fathers, / counsel we learned at our mother's knee. / We're not keeping this to ourselves, / we're passing it along to the next generation— / the marvelous things he has done. / He split the Sea and they walked right through it; / he piled the waters to the right and to the left. / He led them by day with a cloud, / led them all the night long with a fiery torch." (Ps 78:1–4, 13–14, TM)

Journal/Meditation: What sign of divine presence has God created for you? Or what do you use as a sign of the divine presence?

SERVANT

Scripture: "Thus says God, the LORD, / who created the heavens and stretched them out, / who spread out the earth and what comes from it, / who gives breath to the people upon it / and spirit to those who walk in it: / I am the LORD; I have taken you by the hand and kept you." (Isa 42:5–6ac, NRSVue)

Reflection: The concept of something old, something new comes through clearly in Second Isaiah's installation of the servant of God text (Isa 42:1–9), identified by biblical scholars as the first of four servant poems from which the above passage comes. There can be little doubt that the author is relying upon the accounts of creation found in the HB (OT) book of Genesis (1:1—2:25)—the old—and creating a new text from them. First, he combines the two different names for the divine—God (Gen 1:1)—and the LORD (Gen 4:2) to form "God, the LORD" (Isa 42:5a). Second, the heavens, which are fixed above the waters above the dome (Gen 1:7) become like a tent, which is stretched (Isa 42:5b). Third, the earth, a flat plate that goes from a formless void (Gen 1:1) to seas and dry land with vegetation (Gen 1:10–12) becomes like a table spread with all kinds of food. Fourth, from the man into whose nostrils the LORD God breathes the breath of life (Gen 2:7), in Isaiah becomes the breath given to all people upon the earth (Isa 42:5d). And fifth, since the Hebrew word *ruah* can be translated into English as breath, wind, or spirit, Isaiah reiterates that God gives spirit (breath) to the people who walk upon the earth (Isa 42:5d). Thus, the reason for the sending of the servant (Israel) is to instruct humanity about being "a light to the nations" (Isa 42:6c, NRSVue).

The concept of something old, something new also comes through clearly in the last chapter of the OT (A) book of Judith. The female warrior offers a hymn of thanksgiving to God for the defeat of her people's enemy. She sings, "[O Lord, l]et all your creatures serve you, / for you spoke, and they were made. / You sent forth your spirit, and it formed them; / there is none that can resist your voice" (Jdt 16:14, NRSVue). First, the something old is the male warrior, who defeats the enemies of his people; the something new is a woman warrior, who does the same as her male counterpart. Second, the something old are the creatures God makes in Genesis; the something new is that they serve him, like the servant he appoints. As in the first account of creation in the HB (OT) book of Genesis, Judith records that God spoke (Gen 1:24 [old]), and creatures were made (Ps 33:9). Judith adds that their purpose (new) was to serve him. Third, there is nothing in the HB (OT) book of Genesis about God sending forth his spirit to create (old), but there is in Psalm 33:6 and Psalm 104:30, and in Judith (16:14c) (new); however, the Hebrew word *ruah* can be translated into English as *breath*, as well as *spirit*. If it is translated into English as *breath*, then the verse echoes Genesis 2:7. Fourth, Psalm 33:8 emphasizes the LORD's speaking and things coming to be (old), while Judith declares that no one or thing can resist his voice (new) (Jdt 16:14c). Thus, both the HB (OT) book of Second Isaiah and the OT (A) book of Judith present something new being created out of something old.

Psalm Response: "Good people, cheer GOD! / Right-living people sound best when praising. / Invent your own new song to him; / give him a trumpet fanfare. / The skies were made by GOD's command; / he breathed the word and the stars popped out. / He scooped Sea into his jug, / put Ocean in his keg. / Earth-creatures, bow before GOD; / world-dwellers—down on your knees! / Here's why: he spoke and there it was, / in place the moment he said so." (Ps 33:1, 3, 6–9, TM)

Journal/Meditation: In your life, what have you experienced being created new out of something old? Explain.

RIGHTEOUSNESS

Scripture: "Shower, O heavens, from above, / and let the skies rain down righteousness; / let the earth open, that salvation may spring up, / and let it cause righteousness to sprout up also; / I the LORD have created it." (Isa 45:8, NRSVue)

Reflection: Chapter 45 of the Second Prophet Isaiah begins with the LORD choosing King Cyrus of Persia, a world conqueror, to overthrow the power of Babylon and enable the survivors of Judah to return to their homeland. The something old is Judah's exile in Babylon; the something new is a king, who does not know the LORD, becoming his anointed (Is 45:1) or chosen one. Using the weather metaphor, the author of Second Isaiah calls upon the rain to shower righteousness on the earth and, once the rain has soaked into the ground, to let the earth open so that salvation and righteousness spring up. In other words, using old nature, God is creating new salvation and righteousness for his people. Cyrus is the LORD's instrument to deliver the Jews from Babylonian slavery. For that to occur, God must bring righteousness from the heavens to the earth. Like rain giving life to the earth, righteousness seeds are planted and grow. The Hebrew word, *tsedaqah*, can be translated into English as honesty, rightness, moral behavior, fairness, integrity, goodness in everyday life. In other words, righteousness is the quality of being found right or innocent; it is doing the right thing because it is the right thing to do; it is being the right person because it is the right person to be.

King Cyrus of Persia is God's chosen servant. "I am the LORD; I have called you in righteousness; / I have taken you by the hand and kept you; / I have given you as a covenant to the people, / a light to the nations . . ." (Isa 42:6, NRSVue). Like rain launches a process of growth, the LORD, according to Isaiah, has launched a process through the proclamation found in the prophet's words. Righteousness from heaven (rain) takes root as salvation and righteousness on earth, because the LORD has created it in Cyrus. God says, "I have aroused Cyrus in righteousness, / and I will make all his paths straight; he shall . . . set my exiles free . . ." (Isa 45:13, NRSVue). Thus, a pagan king (old) becomes the new liberator of the Jewish exiles in Babylon. Furthermore, a non-Jew is declared to be righteous by the Creator, the LORD, the God of the Jews!

Psalm Response: "Give the gift of wise rule . . . , O God, / the gift of just rule to the crown prince. / May he judge your people rightly . . . . / Be rainfall on cut grass, / earth-refreshing rain showers. / Let righteousness burst into blossom / and peace abound until the moon fades to nothing." (Ps 72:1–2, 6–7, TM)

Journal/Meditation: Are you righteous? Explain. For what have you been chosen by God? Explain the old and new dimensions of your call.

NEW CREATION

Scripture: ". . . I am about to create new heavens and a new earth [says the Lord GOD]; / the former things shall not be remembered or come to mind. / But be glad and rejoice forever in what I am creating, / for I am about to create Jerusalem as a joy and its people as a delight." (Isa 65:17–18, NRSVue)

Reflection: Chapters 55 through 66 of the prophet Isaiah are known as Third Isaiah. They were added to Isaiah after 520–30 BCE, when the return of the Jewish exiles in Babylon had begun or even later. The Scripture passage above reflects that time. God is presented telling the Jews that he is creating everything new; in other words, he is starting over again! The former things—the conquest of Judah by Babylon in 587 BCE and the years in captivity—are over and not to be remembered. In those two verses God is identified as creator three times! Biblically, this is not apocalyptic writing, because there is no destruction of the present heaven and earth. The LORD is at work to make them new. The passage is designed to echo words from Isaiah 48:6b–8b: "From this time forward I tell you new things [says the LORD], / hidden things that you have not known. / They are created now, not long ago; / before today you have never heard of them, / so that you could not say, 'I already knew them.' / You have never heard; you have never known; / from of old your ear has not been opened." In other words, God is creating what was never created and heard of before now.

Like Isaiah before him, the prophet Jeremiah, writing during or after the beginning of the return of the exiles, declares, ". . . [T]he LORD has created a new thing on the earth; a woman encompasses a man" (Jer 31:22). The reference to the woman is Jerusalem encompassing in her walls the returnees. For both prophets, God is transforming the cosmos; out of something old—destroyed Kingdom of Judah and demolished holy city Jerusalem—God is creating something new. The LORD is in control.

Psalm Response: "God, it seems you've been our home forever; / long before the mountains were born. / So don't return us to mud, saying, / 'Back to where you came from!' / Patience! You've got all the time in the world— whether / a thousand years or a day, it's all the same to you. / Are we no more to you than a wispy dream, / no more than a blade of grass / That springs up gloriously with the rising sun / and is cut down without a second thought? / We live for seventy years or so / (with luck we might make it to eighty) . . . . / Oh! Teach us to live well! / Teach us to live wisely and well!" (Ps 90:1, 3–6, 10, 12, TM)

Journal/Meditation: In your lifetime, what new heavens and new earth have you witnessed God creating? Explain. From what old did the new emerge?

NEW HUMANITY

Scripture: ". . . [I]n [Christ Jesus'] flesh he has made both [Gentiles and Jews] into one and has broken down the dividing wall, that is, the hostility between us, abolishing the law with its commandments and ordinances, that he might create in himself one new humanity in place of the two . . . ." (Eph 2:14–15, NRSVue)

Reflection: The Letter to the Ephesians is a second-generation Pauline biblical book written by an author who understood genuine Pauline thought and sought to explain and distribute it far and wide. The unknown author presents the division that existed in the first century CE. People belonged to either of two groups: Gentiles and Jews. Gentiles did not practice circumcision; Jews did circumcise male children on the eighth day after their birth. In the view of both Paul and his second-generation expositor, this created two different groups of people, best illustrated by the wall separating Jews and pious Gentiles in the Jerusalem Temple. Before Jesus, Jews tried to convert Gentiles to their way of life, and Gentiles resisted primarily because of circumcision and the requirement of adhering to the 613 precepts of Torah. However, according to Paul (Gal 3:28), God's raising of Jesus from the dead has created a new humanity. The time of keeping Torah has passed (not good news to Jews, but good news to male Gentiles). In the resurrected body of Christ Jesus, with the elimination of Torah the two different groups have become one new humanity.

The God who created the chosen people has decided to choose all people! He has taken what was old, and in Christ Jesus created a new self, created according to the likeness of God (Eph 4:24), just like he did originally (Gen 1:27; 2:7). In the words of Ephesians, no one is a stranger or alien (2:19); all are now fellow citizens or members of God's household. All have access in the Spirit to the Father (Eph 2:18) and all are constructed spiritually into a dwelling place for God (Eph 2:22). Paul had had a breakthrough moment that radically changed his thinking; out of something old (Gentiles and Jews) God created a new single humanity through Christ Jesus. Paul's follower (the unknown author of Ephesians) explained the transformative moment, explained its consequences, and applied it to people living near the end of the first century CE.

Psalm Response: "Hallelujah! / Praise [God] for his acts of power, / praise him for his magnificent greatness; / Praise with a blast on the trumpet, / praise by strumming soft strings; / Praise him with castanets and dance, / praise him with banjo and flute; / Praise him with cymbals and a big bass drum, / praise him with fiddles and mandolin. / Let every living, breathing creature praise GOD! / Hallelujah! (Ps 150:1a, 3–6)

Journal/Meditation: What dividing wall among people do you think still needs to be demolished to unite humanity? In what specific ways do commandments and ordinances get in the way of accomplishing the new humanity?

Summary

In this chapter on creation, something old became something new. An old cloud became the sign of divine presence. Old Judah and Jerusalem, destroyed by the Babylonians, was renewed by the return of the Jewish exiles. Not only did they become something new, but the LORD covered them with his divine protection. His people, identified as his collective servant, he filled with breath or spirit to form from an exiled people a new creation. The path from exile to freedom clearly illustrates the something old being created into something new. The old nature of the people was changed by God into righteousness; the quality of being found right or innocent replaced guilt. Salvation sprouted from a pagan king chosen by the LORD to liberate his people. From the old Judah and Jerusalem, from the old heavens and earth, the LORD created a new Judah and Jerusalem and new heavens and new earth. In other words, transformation took place. In the Christian Bible (New Testament), a second-generation Pauline author reiterated his teacher, stating that in Christ Jesus God had created a new humanity. No longer would there be Jews and Gentiles; one new humanity had brought them together. Furthermore, with the end of Torah observance, all Jews and Gentiles had been transformed (re-created) into one new humanity. Thus, the biblical process of creation that had occurred in the HB (OT) book of Genesis, which had resulted in separation, after separation, after separation had been re-created to be one, as the biblical authors presumed God had intended from the beginning.

Recent Books by Mark G. Boyer Published by Wipf & Stock

Nature Spirituality: Praying with Wind, Water, Earth, Fire

A Spirituality of Ageing

Weekday Saints: Reflections on Their Scriptures

Human Wholeness: A Spirituality of Relationship

A Simple Systematic Mariology

Praying Your Way through Luke's Gospel and the Acts of the Apostles

An Abecedarian of Animal Spirit Guides: Spiritual Growth through Reflections on Creatures

Overcome with Paschal Joy: Chanting through Lent and Easter—Daily Reflections with Familiar Hymns

Taking Leave of Your Home: Moving in the Peace of Christ

An Abecedarian of Sacred Trees: Spiritual Growth through Reflections on Woody Plants

Divine Presence: Elements of Biblical Theophanies

Fruit of the Vine: A Biblical Spirituality of Wine

Names for Jesus: Reflections for Advent and Christmas

Talk to God and Listen to the Casual Reply: Experiencing the Spirituality of John Denver

Christ Our Passover Has Been Sacrificed: A Guide through Paschal Mystery Spirituality—Mystical Theology in The Roman Missal

Rosary Primer: The Prayers, The Mysteries, and the New Testament

Recent Books by Mark G. Boyer Published by Wipf & Stock

From Contemplation to Action: The Spiritual Process of Divine Discernment Using Elijah and Elisha as Models

Love Addict

All Things Mary: Honoring the Mother of God—An Anthology of Marian Reflections

Shhh! The Sound of Sheer Silence: A Biblical Spirituality that Transforms

What is Born of the Spirit is Spirit: A Biblical Spirituality of Spirit

Very Short Reflections—for Advent and Christmas, Lent and Easter, Ordinary Time, and Saints—through the Liturgical Year

Living Parables: Today's Versions

My Life of Ministry, Writing, Teaching, and Traveling: The Autobiography of an Old Mines Missionary

300 Years of the French in Old Mines: A Narrative History of the Oldest Village in Missouri

Journey into God: Spiritual Reflections for Travelers

Monthly Entries for the Spiritual but not Religious through the Year: Texts, Reflections, Journal/Meditations, and Prayers for the Spiritual but not Religious

The Shelbydog Chronicles by Shelby Cole as Recorded by Mark G. Boyer: A Novel

Four Catholic Pioneers in Missouri: Lamarque, Kenrick, Fox, and Hogan: Irish Missionaries and Their Supporter

Smothered with Inexhaustible Mercy: An Anthology of Poems

Spirituality for the Solitary: A Handbook for Those Who Live Alone

Seasons of Biblical Spirituality: Spring, Summer, Autumn, Winter

Biblical Names for God: An Abecedarian Anthology of Spiritual Reflections for Anytime

More Shelbydog Chronicles: Reflections on a Dog's Life by Her Friend, Knowing Your Pet

His Mercy Endures Forever: Biblical Reflections on Divine Mercy for Anytime

The Roman Catholic Lectionary and the Bible: Analysis, Conclusions, Suggested Alternatives

The Spirit of the Lord God: Biblical Names and Images for the Holy Spirit; An Abecedarian Anthology of Spiritual Reflections for Anytime

A Biblical Morning & Evening Prayer Manual: A Modern Book of Hours, Ways to Begin and End the Day

The Folks in the Woods: A Memoir of Brown Hollow, Missouri, 1874–1991

The Liturgical Environment: What the Documents Say about Roman Catholic Churches, Fourth Edition, Updated and Revised

Eavesdropping on Paul: Reading Others' Biblical Mail

www.ingramcontent.com/pod-product-compliance
Lightning Source LLC
Chambersburg PA
CBHW061513040426
42450CB00008B/1593